AF696022

Personality Traits of Electronic Cigarette Quitters

Mohd Rashid

Abstract

Increasingly, e-cigarettes are being used and claimed to be an effective means of smoking cessation. Clinical studies have been limited to the aspects of use pertaining to chemical dependence, yet little addiction research has examined the psychology of smoking cessation behavior utilizing e-cigarettes. Health behaviors, such as harm reduction in smoking through the use of nicotine replacement therapies, have been previously studied and several dispositional traits have been found to be highly related to these behaviors. These personality factors include Neuroticism and Conscientiousness, Self-Efficacy, Grit, and Hardiness. The present study aimed to determine psychological traits related to successful smoking cessation utilizing e-cigarettes using measures of NEO-FFI-3, GSE, DRS-II, and Grit-S. Results indicated that Self-Efficacy was a noteworthy factor associated with cessation with 6 months or more of e-cigarette use. A majority of the study participants did not concurrently smoke and use e-cigarettes. These findings support the potential of e-cigarettes as a replacement therapy and provide some insight into formulating interventions toward this end; however, smoking cessation attempts appeared to be inhibited from full success as a result of the efficacy of the replacement.

Table of Contents

Chapter 1: Nature of the Study

Background of the Problem

Among substance use disorders, the assessment and treatment of cigarette smoking has been highlighted in public health extensively and widely studied. Smoking has been characterized by both chemical and behavioral aspects delineated along lines of active use, withdrawal, and craving that activate neurological reward pathways and reinforce its addictive nature. Treatment approaches encompass detoxification, reducing harmful use, and recovery through abstinence often punctuated by relapse. Personality factors that play roles in both the susceptibility to and resiliency in addiction. One relatively recent treatment approach involves the use of electronic cigarettes for harm reduction and cessation. The potential in reducing overall mortality warrants examination of the health behavior of adopting these devices. Identifying personality correlates in this process may inform future treatment strategies.

Health Impact

Cigarette smoking is a prominent public health concern. It was elucidated in the 1964 Surgeon General's report (U.S. Department of Health, Education, and Welfare, 1964) as “associated with a 70 percent increase in the age-specific death rates... [and increasing] the risk of dying from chronic bronchitis and emphysema” (pp.31, 82) as well as lung cancer, cardiovascular disease, low infant birth weight, also accidental death. The report identified smoking habituation and occasional discontinuation as psychologically and socially determined not excepting physiological factors especially related to habituation, nor predisposition or genetic factors. That tobacco smoking had been extolled for curative value for hundreds of years was attributed in part to the alkaloid nicotine which the pharmacology and chronic toxicity in doses comparable to the amounts absorbable from cigarette smoking or other use of tobacco products were evaluated as a health hazard based on the direct, reflex, and chemical mediator effects of nicotine on autonomic nervous transmission and organic excitability. Departing from demographic factors ranging widely, it was suggested that among other personality traits Extraversion as well Neuroticism had been associated with the habit pattern of smoking although the broad categorization of heterogeneous smokers' behavior obscured clear relationships.

Doweiko (2012) cited research that had isolated some 4,700 chemicals from cigarette smoke, including nicotine- the primary reinforcing agent and psychoactive compound in tobacco, which strong evidence has suggested is added by manufacturers to the content already present. Inhalation of cigarette smoke was found to contain compounds such as acetone, ammonia, arsenic, benzene, carbon monoxide, hydrogen cyanide, lead, and tar or burnt plant resins among others; furthermore, it was argued that little research had been conducted on the toxicological effects of these compounds in the human body. Additionally, as tobacco plants grow environmental pollutants are concentrated in the leaves which in turn are processed into cigarettes for consumption and represent another potential chemical danger of cigarette smoke. It was asserted that there is a consensus that there is no “safe” cigarette.

Pharmacology

Because cigarettes account for 90% of all tobacco use in the United States (Inaba & Cohen, 2007), there is considerable need to examine its use objectively. The addictive potential of smoking has been characterized by poor outcomes despite negative health consequences with cessation programs yielding 20% abstinence for one year in some cases while self-assisted efforts have been found to have poorer success, approximately 4% abstaining for 6 months (Carlson, 2010). As a chemical of dependence, nicotine and its effects on the central nervous system have been previously studied.

Nicotine is a parasympathomimetic alkaloid that acts as a central nervous system stimulant. The chemical stimulates nicotinic acetylcholine (ACh) receptors and increases activity of dopaminergic neurons of the mesolimbic system, releasing dopamine (DA) in the nucleus accumbens (NAcc; Carlson, 2010). Nicotine mimics ACh, which affects heart rate, blood pressure, learning, memory, reflexes, aggression, sleep, and mental acuity among other processes, by slotting into receptor sites and exaggerating cholinergic effects while the release of DA causes feelings of satisfaction and calmness; therefore, cigarette use both stimulates and tranquilizes (Inaba & Cohen, 2007). This dual effect contributes to the addictiveness of cigarettes.

The reinforcing effect of nicotine is caused by the activation of receptors in the ventral tegmental area (VTA; Carlson, 2010). Neuronal levels of transmitters during acute intoxication were characterized by increased catecholamines, such as DA, and decreased reuptake which caused increased activity that preceded acute withdrawal which due to depletion and reduced reuptake was characterized by feelings of craving, depression, and restlessness (Preston, O'Neal, & Talaga, 2010) associated with a desensitized state during which ACh binded to receptors but did not react which in turn stimulated the an increase in the numbers of nicotinic receptors (Carlson, 2010). Nicotine-induced DA release is enhanced by decreased monoamine oxidase levels which caused dopaminergic effect at saturated receptor sites where it binded to be stronger and more prolonged as a result of slower DA reuptake and was associated with increased release of vasopressin, GABA, glutamate, and epinephrine involved in the sensation of relaxation or pleasure as well as alertness (Doweiko, 2012). Reduced catecholamine levels produce a state of desensitization induced by long-term binding at ACh receptors where the process of resensitization begins almost immediately while receptor sites are not occupied by nicotine molecules (Doweiko, 2012) and chronic use develops tolerance, further reduced availability of neurotransmitters, and supersensitivity caused by an increased number of receptors leading to exacerbated withdrawal symptoms (Preston et al., 2010). The cycle between cigarette consumption and smoking another cigarette produces an approximately 45-minute period of desensitization which can be protracted by continued nicotine administration throughout a day, causing a feeling of relaxation as a result of smoking that contributes to craving when a smoker interrupts this cycle (Doweiko, 2012).

Cessation after long-term use causes withdrawal symptoms of anxiety, restlessness, insomnia, and inability to concentrate which may increase the likelihood of relapse as a result of deficient homeostatic activation of the medial prefrontal cortex and NAcc in smokers (Carlson, 2010). Peak nicotine concentrations achieved within the first few minutes of smoking, which decreases as nicotine is redistributed to body tissues, was biotransformed but not depleted and resulted in an accumulation of nicotine constantly renewed while a smoker continues to smoke led to a change in brain metabolism that interfered with cortical and subcortical processing of the integration and expression of emotions with perceptions (Doweiko, 2012). Tolerance is rapidly lost during night hours when nicotine receptors again become sensitized, entering back into an acute withdrawal state during the period of abstinence, which consequently causes the first dose in the morning to produce a strong effect of pleasure via the reinforcing effect (Carlson, 2010; Doweiko, 2012) accompanied by increases in heart rate and blood pressure (Inaba & Cohen, 2007). In this way, a pattern of use characterized by nicotine blood-level fluctuations and associated ACh and DA receptor saturation activates the endogenous reward system of the limbic system.

Addiction

Smoking abstinence stimulates the number of nicotinic receptors in the brain to return to normal, but the high rate of relapse has indicated that craving persists and implicates the occurrence of related brain changes (Carlson, 2010). Addiction has been defined as a chronic, relapsing brain disease characterized by compulsive drug seeking and use despite harmful consequences (National Institutes of Health [NIH], 2008). The physiological basis of addiction was described by Carlson (2010) as the reinforcing effects of addictive substances, positive reinforcement when a behavior is regularly followed by an appetitive stimulus—one that an organism will approach—with faster-acting substance effects establishing dependence more quickly, which is associated with the stimulation of dopamine release in the NAcc from neural changes in the excitatory synapses of the VTA, and negative reinforcement when a behavior is followed by a reduction or termination of an aversive stimulus, for example, the reduction of withdrawal effects; notwithstanding, craving – the urge to use an addictive substance again—cannot be completely explained by withdrawal effects alone rather the ventromedial prefrontal cortex has been found to play an inhibitory role in reinstatement while the dorsal anterior cingulate cortex played a facilitatory role, long-term substance abuse was associated with decreased activity of the prefrontal cortex and decreased volume of prefrontal gray matter which impairs judgment and the ability to inhibit inappropriate choices.

Historically, the medicalization of this pattern produced the disease model of addiction (Jellinek, 1960) and this conceptualization continued to challenge diagnosis on the basis of symptom clustering. The term *addiction* was supplanted by *dependence* to describe compulsive drug-seeking behavior in the *Diagnostic and Statistics Manual of Mental Disorders* (DSM) *III-R* (American Psychiatric Association [APA], 1987). Critiques of criterion symptoms for dependence, which were restricted to persistent psychoactive substance use, suggested that these terms could aptly apply to other forms of repetitive behaviors (Collins, 1991); however, the focus on substance-related addiction persisted in DSM-IV-TR (APA, 2000), which characterized dependence by the presence within a 12-month period of at least three of the following symptoms: (a) tolerance, as indicated by the need for a markedly increased amount of the substance to achieve the desired effect or a markedly diminished effect with continued use of the same amount; (b) withdrawal symptoms, or use of the substance to avoid withdrawal symptoms; (c) greater intake of the substance or use over a longer period of time than intended; (d) a persistent desire or unsuccessful attempts to limit substance use; (e) an inordinate amount of time spent on activities related to obtaining the substance, using the substance, or recovering from its effects; (f) giving up or reducing important social, occupational, or recreational activities because of substance use; and (g) continued use of the substance despite knowledge of its having persistent negative physiological or psychological effects.

Orford (2001) offered the excessive appetite model of addiction, a comprehensive model including principally excessive drinking, smoking, gambling, eating, sex, and the diverse range of substances in a broader conceptualization consisting of very skewed consumption distribution curves; restraint, control or deterrence; positive incentive learning mechanisms highlighting rapid emotional change as rewards and wide cue conditioning; complex memory schemata; secondary acquired emotional regulation; as well as related issues in other major areas of functioning, these processes in turn resulting in strong attachment to appetitive activity such that self-control is diminished or that behavior might appear disease-like. The compulsive nature of addiction is such that the reward system might register a relatively rapid and substantial improvement in hedonic state that cannot be obtained otherwise, thus the performance of the addictive behavior leads to maladaptive functioning and a state of chronic dysphoria (Lemon, 2002). There is support for a conceptualization of addiction as a pattern of behavior not restricted to the use of psychoactive substances.

The use of the term *dependence* has been perceived as too closely related to physical dependence and withdrawal, which has prompted a clinical preference to revert to *addiction* and the connotation of loss of control over cravings despite consequences (APA, 2008). A critique of the DSM-IV-TR conceptualization which notably excluded behavioral addictions that were not recognized due to the notion that addictions occur exclusively on a physiological level, conflict over the definition of recovery from these addictive disorders, and the assumption that the behaviors might better be accounted for by other disorders; in response, it has been argued that the behaviors as a form of interaction rather than a substance on which the body can become dependent prove exception to the limitation of substance-induced addiction, total abstinence in the recovery process as analogous treatment goals between the two, and the lack of criterion validity with respect to the impulsive or obsessive-compulsive causing harm to the person engaging in the behavior or to others, which is not always the case, thus supporting a need for a distinct diagnosis (Hagedorn, 2009). Frascella et al. (2010) afforded neurobiological data, i.e. that in the case of gambling similar ventral striatum and orbitofrontal cortex activation contribute to pathological gambling urges as in stimulant dependence; the case of obesity implicating the same mesolimbic dopamine system in compulsive or excessive eating as with substance abuse particularly the midbrain VTA projections to the NAcc as well as the amygdala, ventral striatum, hippocampus, and medial prefrontal cortex; and the case of sex, a biological imperative with associated arousal and orgasm likewise affecting the mesolimbic reward system via amygdala, ventral striatum, medial prefrontal cortex, and orbitofrontal cortex which are also implicated in substance abuse, and hypothalamic control of sex hormones e.g. testosterone can induce obsessive thoughts about sex, supporting a need to recognize these shared brain vulnerabilities as indicator that nosologic boundaries be extended to better encompass addictions as a distinct diagnostic category.

DSM 5 (APA, 2013) revisions expanded the category of substance-related disorders to include addictive disorders, groups of repetitive behaviors sometimes called behavioral addictions, which activate reward systems similar to those activated by substances of abuse and produce symptoms that appear comparable to those produced by substance use disorders. Inaba and Cohen (2007) characterized smoking as a "pure example" of the addictive process, the pleasure received from the direct effects of smoking being less intense than other chemicals and the negative feelings from early tobacco use commonly outweighing pleasurable ones and rare identification of the first use as pleasurable yet persistent high addiction potential. Smoking involves both direct effects of a substance as well as behavioral features that themselves have diagnostic significance. Withdrawal symptoms of sleep disturbance, irritability, difficulties in concentration, restlessness, gastrointestinal upset, and cravings from cessation typically begin within 2 hours, peak within 24 hours, and gradually decline in intensity over 10 days (Doweiko, 2012).

Altered brain metabolism in the NAcc region is conducive to the stimulated release of endogenous compounds most akin to the opiod family that the greater the exposure, the higher chance of a chemical addiction to nicotine (Doweiko, 2012). The reinforcing effect during use and as a result of cravings motivate repetitive drug-seeking behavior, which itself activates neural reward pathways. In this way, smoking is associated with a pattern of substance and non-substance factors contributing to addiction. The DSM 5 lists three disorders that applicably characterize smoking which are tobacco use disorder, tobacco withdrawal, or otherwise related diagnosis as well as the diagnostic category of non-substance related disorders.

A predisposition to substance abuse is an explanation for the etiology of addictive behaviors which posits that in individuals with such a predisposition the same brain changes occur with substance use as with addictive behaviors. Genetic predispositions have been more recently examined in a variety of chemical addictions (Inaba & Cohen, 2007). A widely studied theoretical approach to personality predispositions is the negative reinforcement model, which suggests that the primary basis of motivation for addiction is the reduction or avoidance of negative affective states (Baker et al., 2004). It has been found that relapse can be predicted with some accuracy by brain imaging. Clark et al. (2014) identified smaller absolute blood oxygen level-dependent response amplitude in the following two areas: bilateral ventral posterior cingulate, a region associated with the limbic system and involved in processing self-relevant information which a deficit could result in increased difficulty in maintaining abstinence due to a lack of predictive understanding regarding harmful effects of a decisions; and the right insular cortex, a region associated with the assessment of emotionally aversive environmental conditions modulated by perceptual awareness of threat and penalty, which is also associated with smoking cessation after legions. Personality structures affecting these neurological referents have been studied in the context of the negative reinforcement model. For example, trait aggression which has been psychometrically established as a negative affective trait was found to predispose individuals with low distress tolerance to alcohol use that in response to negative affect brought perceived or real relief thereby reinforcing the behavior and increasing the likelihood of continued use in the future (Bina et al., 2013). The diminished ability to distinguish between alternatives leading to beneficial or detrimental outcomes characteristic of addiction appear to be modulated by innate personality features. Other personality factors that have been investigated for roles in negative health outcomes include Impulsivity (MacKillop, 2013), Curiosity (Jovanović & Gavrilov-Jerković, 2014), Conscientiousness and Neuroticism (Tucker, Elliott & Klein, 2006), among others.

Mortality

Smoking, known to cause cancer of the mouth, throat, larynx, blood, lungs, stomach, pancreas, kidney, bladder and cervix, is linked to an estimated 440,000 deaths per year (NIH, 2008). The same carcinogens hazardous to human health that affect smokers also affect non-smokers. It has been found that there is an up to 30% increase in risk of both lung cancer and coronary heart disease from secondhand smoke exposure as well as other respiratory effects, developmental impacts, and cardiovascular issues (Doweiko, 2012; U.S. Department of Health and Human Services, 2006). It has been found that one person dies from secondhand smoke for every eight smoker deaths (Inaba & Cohen, 2007), a proportion of which consists of children (Doweiko, 2012). Smoking poses serious health risks for individual smokers and proximal individuals alike.

Health Behavior

Behaviors which affect the health of an individual who engages in them are termed health behaviors. The primary effect of these behaviors is on an individual's own health and may influence the health of others indirectly, such as in the case of smoking in which the behavior affects a smoker's health as well as proximal others' by secondhand smoke (Simons-Martin, 2013). Self-protective behaviors are undertaken in a purposeful manner to prevent risk of illness or harm (Kasl & Cobb, 1996) with moderating effects from substantial physical and social influences as well as genetics and environmental factors that precede cognitions and condition behavior over time (Simons-Martin, 2013). The motivations to quit smoking has been characterized as being a direct outcome of perceptions of personal health risk, severity of personal susceptibility, and a perception of the benefits of cessation being higher and costs lower than continuation in addition to the intentionality and intensity resultant of a desire to comply with normative perceptions of sources including others and the social environment (Manfredi et al., 1998). Seeking treatment or self-assisted attempts to quit may be conceptualized as health behaviors that smokers adopt toward cessation.

Smoking Cessation

Abstaining from cigarettes and quitting long-term constitutes smoking cessation. The ultimate goal of cessation programs is the extinction of nicotine substance use and the behavioral aspects that reinforce its use. Among smokers, some 80% have tried to quit at least once; however, it has been found that on average 5-10 quit attempts are made before successful cessation and of the 34% of current smokers who attempt to quit each year only 2.5% discontinue use during each attempt (Doweiko, 2012). Smoking cessation is clearly a difficult goal despite salient health reasons.

The Transtheoretical Model of Change (Prochaska & DiClemente, 1983) has been used as a framework for conceptualizing the health behavior of smoking cessation (Prochaska, 1996). In this model intention and behavior are measured according to the following five stages of change: precontemplation, in which there is no intention to change in the next 6 months; contemplation, in which there is an intention to take action in the same time frame; preparation, in which there is intention to change behavior within a month; action, the stage in which a new behavior has been adopted and maintained for less than 6 months; and the maintenance stage, in which the behavior has been maintained for more than 6 months (Prochaska, Redding & Evers, 2002). A core construct of this process is Self-Efficacy, the confidence an individual has in the ability to take action in difficult situations, and it has been found that behavioral strategies such as helping relationships, counter-conditioning, reinforcement management, stimulus control, and self-liberation have a significant relationship with progression through stages of change (Ham, 2007).

There are many benefits of quitting. Inaba and Cohen (2007) enumerated the following: within 20 minutes of quitting blood pressure, pulse, and temperature return to normal; within 8 hours, blood levels of carbon monoxide decrease and oxygen levels increase; within 24 hours, risk of sudden heart attack decreases; within 48 hours, nerve transmission adjusts to the absence of nicotine and senses of smell and taste begin to normalize; within 1 week, breathing improves and constricted blood vessels begin to relax; within 2 to 12 weeks, circulation and lung function improve; within 1 to 9 months, symptoms of fatigue, coughing, sinus congestion, and shortness of breath decrease; within 1 year the risk of coronary heart disease decreases to half that of a smoker; within 5 years, heart disease death rate is equal to that of a non-smoker and lung cancer death rate decreases by 50% and to that of a non-smoker within 10 years; and within 10-15 years the risk of all major diseases caused by smoking decreases to nearly that of an individual who has never smoked. Despite immediate physiological impact associated with smoking cessation, the persistence of craving makes smoking addiction highly vulnerable to relapse.

Clinical Treatment

Pharmacological treatment along with psychosocial therapies are considered essential to improve outcomes (Diaper, Law, & Melichar, 2013). Levels of care may range from detoxification, inpatient hospitalization, residential treatment, outpatient programs, or self-help (Ruiz et al., 2007). Pharmacological intervention is often utilized to assist in early intervention and maintenance. An integrated treatment plan should be formulated jointly with a physician to enable patient self-regulated drug therapy, if possible. Regardless of such efficacy, individuals being treated for physical dependence often initiate drug-seeking behaviors anyway (Hedrickson et al., 2004). An interdisciplinary approach to treating addiction is generally promoted.

Neuronal responses to pharmacotherapy for treatment of nicotine addiction have been previously studied. Carlson (2010) cited research findings that injections of nicotinic agonist into the VTA led to conditioned reinforcement, while injections of nicotinic antagonist into the VTA reduced the reinforcing effect but not when injected into the NAcc despite presence of receptors in both and that this VTA mechanism was attributed to action preventing the release of DA in the NAcc. Endogenous craving has been found to be caused by depletion of DA activity at the NAcc (Inaba & Cohen, 2007). Given these characteristics, pharmacotherapies for nicotine detoxification are delineated in two broad approaches of treating withdrawal symptoms and nicotine replacement therapy (NRT). Partial agonists are utilized to counteract withdrawal symptoms and reduce smoking satisfaction which can be useful for long-term cessation (Diaper et al., 2013). Drugs that are commonly employed include varenicline, clonidine, mecamylamine (APA, 2008; Diaper et al., 2013; Preston et al., 2010) in conjunction with second line antidepressants such as fluoxetine, paroxetine, sertraline, venlafaxine (Diaper et al., 2013) as well as buproprion, nortriptyline, MAOIs (APA, 2008; Preston et al., 2010) and non-nicotine drugs, i.e. naltrexone, rimonabant, tiagabine, and GABA-based drugs (APA, 2008; Diaper et al., 2013).

The purpose of NRT is to reduce the blood plasma nicotine level to a degree that cessation will not trigger severe withdrawal symptoms and not reinforce addiction, a maintenance process of preventing relapse sometimes called antipriming (Inaba & Cohen, 2007).

Delivery systems include nicotine-containing gum, transdermal patches, lozenges, and prescription vapor inhalers or nasal sprays (APA, 2008; Doweiko, 2012; Inaba & Cohen, 2007). These treatments directly stimulate nicotine ACh receptors and reduce the urge to smoke, withdrawal effects, and reward from cigarettes during relapse (Diaper et al., 2013). NRT limits exposure to other chemicals produced from smoking and further allows for a gradual reduction of nicotine dosage over an extended period of time (Doweiko, 2012). These methods of nicotine delivery provide a less harmful, less reinforcing administration than smoking and have been found to improve cessation rates by 50-70% (Diaper et al., 2013) although some estimates suggest quit rates increase by up to 150% the rate with placebo (APA, 2008). NRT regimen for detoxification is recommended to be initiated two weeks before a cessation attempt and to have a duration of a minimum of eight weeks, or for as long as necessary (Diaper et al., 2013). The failure rate of pharmacological treatments is extremely high, estimates of recidivism ranging from 62-89% (Inaba & Cohen, 2007), and have been explained by less efficient delivery of nicotine than through smoking as well as by not mimicking the behavioral rituals associated with smoking (Diaper et al., 2013). Compromised effectiveness for cessation from pharmacotherapy alone supports collateral utilization of additional interventions.

A common practice is the integration of psychotherapeutic intervention to assist in long-term recovery (Inaba & Cohen, 2007; APA, 2008; Preston et al., 2010; Doweiko, 2012; Diaper et al., 2013). Along with relapse prevention counseling and self-help groups in conjunction with NRT increase the success of treatment (Inaba & Cohen, 2007). Self-help materials impart cessation skills via community support, cognitive behavioral therapy may be utilized to develop cognitive coping strategies to manage triggers, and motivational enhancement therapy promotes self-motivation thereby increasing intention for smoking cessation (APA, 2008). It has also been considered whether or not hypnotherapy can effectively aid smoking cessation by acting on underlying impulses to weaken desire to smoke and strengthen the will to abstain (Barnes et al., 2010). A wide variety of therapeutic approaches can support health behavior in smoking cessation.

Harm Reduction

Detoxification has been framed as a transitional state between addiction and abstinence characterized by a reduction of harm (Diaper et al., 2013). Harm reduction is a model of addiction treatment based on the principle of changing behavior over time with the goal of diminishing immediate consequences of use, or perhaps consequences of doing in the case of an addictive behavior, rather than attempting to support abstinence at least initially (APA, 2008; Doweiko, 2012). NRT represents a harm reduction process for smoking. Many individuals have difficulty stopping the NRT that was used for smoking cessation (Doweiko, 2012); however, the continued use of the replacement is less harmful than cigarette smoking as a result of the absence of the myriad of chemicals found in cigarette smoke beside nicotine and therefore preferable. There has been a recent influx of scientific research, including numerous epidemiological studies, over the past 10 years on harm reduction in the context of smoking in particular (Rodu, 2011).

One NRT not previously mentioned is the use of electronic cigarettes (e-cigarettes). These devices consist of a power source which activates an atomizer that heats a aqueous solution of glycerol that contains flavoring and varying concentrations of nicotine, although some have no nicotine content, producing a vapor which is inhaled. This method of nicotine delivery does not produce secondhand smoke nor does it expose a user to the variety of cursory constituents from combusting tobacco, thus making it less harmful than smoking (Doweiko,

2012). It has been suggested that e-cigarettes hold tremendous promise in harm reduction of tobacco-related morbidity and mortality (Cahn & Siegel, 2011). Some debate has arisen over the use of e-cigarettes in smoking cessation. A brief review ensues.

E-Cigarettes

It has been suggested that e-cigarettes have potential to decrease morbidity and mortality related to smoking. E-cigarette use has continued to increase in recent years (Farsalinos, Romagna, Tsiapras, Kyrzopoulos, & Voudris, 2014; King et al., 2013). Approximately 1 in 5 current smokers reported having ever used e-cigarettes (King et al, 2013). There is no evidence that large numbers of non-smokers will use e-cigarettes and become addicted to nicotine (Polosa et al., 2013). E-cigarettes were mostly used as a long-term substitute to avoid harm associated with smoking and were reportedly effective even in highly-dependent smokers (Farsalinos, Romagna, et al., 2014). Smokers unable or unwilling to quit may switch to e-cigarettes as a safer alternative and possible pathway to cessation (Hajek et al., 2014). E-cigarettes eliminate the smoke toxicants responsible for nearly all smoking-related diseases; therefore, abuse liability is a moot point in the context of harm reduction (Polosa et al., 2013). Side effects of use appear to be minor, health benefits substantial (Farsalinos, Romagna, et al., 2014).

Immediate physiological effects have been laboratory tested. It was found that the hemodynamic parameters affected by cigarette smoking were not affected by e-cigarette use, perhaps due to the impact of carbon monoxide contained in smoke but not in vapor (Czogala et al., 2012). Whereas smoking caused a delay in myocardial relaxation, the use of e-cigarettes did not (Farsalinos, Tsiapras, Kyrzopoulos, Savvopoulou, & Voudris, 2014). In addition, e-cigarette use did not influence complete blood count indices, whereas smoking was found to increase the secondary proteins of acute inflammatory load for at least one hour (Flouris et al., 2012).

Significant elevations in carboxyhemoglobin and coronary vascular resistance index as well as decrease in coronary flow velocity reserve observed in smokers was absent after e-cigarette use (Farsalinos, Tsiapras, et al, 2013). After two weeks of use, another study found decreased arterial and venous carboxyhemoglobin levels as well as an increase in oxygen saturation among smokers who converted to e-cigarettes (van Staden et al., 2013). There was no evidence of abnormal blood pressure, hematological data or blood chemistry and no severe adverse events were observed in a separate four week trial (Miura et al., 2011). Direct positive effects have been strongly endorsed with very low reporting of adverse effects (Dawkins & Corcoran, 2014).

E-cigarette users typically use high levels of nicotine at initiation and subsequently try to reduce nicotine consumption, with a small minority using non-nicotine liquids (Farsalinos, Romagna, et al., 2014). It was reported that e-cigarettes did not deliver nicotine effectively after acute administration (Eissenberg, 2010). Indeed, only 50-60% of nicotine content appeared to have been vaporized in one study (Goniecwicz et al., 2013); moreover, plasma nicotine levels were higher by 35-72% when using new- compared to first-generation devices, although still only delivering one-third to one-fourth the amount of nicotine compared to tobacco cigarettes (Farsalinos, Spyrou, et al., 2014). There appears to be variability between devices. Other studies reported a significant rise in plasma nicotine concentration (Vansickel & Eissenberg, 2013; Dawkins & Corcoran, 2014; Nides et al., 2014). Acute effects of administration in another study did not include measurable levels of nicotine or carbon monoxide concentrations, but did suppress nicotine abstinence symptom ratings (Vansickel et al., 2010); however, cotinine, a metabolite of nicotine, has been found in substantial amounts in the saliva of e-cigarette users similar to the levels observed in smokers (Etter & Bullen, 2011b). In fact, cotinine levels were found to decrease in smokers after two weeks of e-cigarette use (van Staden et al., 2013). It has been found that the inhaled amount of nicotine per puff is lower compared with a conventional cigarette (Goniewicz, Kuma, et al., 2013). The concern over low nicotine delivery was countered by evidence that despite such data e-cigarettes provide significant craving reduction (Wagener, Siegel & Borrelli, 2012). Notwithstanding, the conclusion that e-cigarettes do not reliably increase blood nicotine levels may be resultant of methodological inconsistencies, such as the recruitment of e-cigarette-naïve users as respondents or failure to control for puffing topography during use (Etter & Bullen, 2011b).

Regarding the vaporizing fluid itself, there was very little risk of nicotine toxicity from major brands of e-cigarettes because nicotine content in the vaporization liquid was not well related to nicotine in vapor, and variations in concentration across batches of a given liquid was low (Goniewicz, Hajek, & McRobbie, 2013). Nicotine content was close to label statements (Etter, Zäther, & Svennsson, 2013). There was, however, reported presence of metal and silicate particles in fluid and aerosol in amounts probably greater than a conventional cigarette user would experience, which likely resulted from the manufacturing process (Williams et al., 2013; Saffari et al., 2014). Several fluid brands contained detectable impurities above the levels set for nicotine products, but below the level likely to cause harm (Etter et al., 2013). In fact, a large proportion of sweet-flavored liquids were found to contain diacetyl and acetyl propionyl, chemicals approved for food use but associated with respiratory disease when inhaled, at levels higher than the safety limits (Farsalinos, Kistler, et al., 2014). Cytotoxicity has been found to be related to the number and concentration of chemicals used to flavor these liquids (Bahl et al., 2012; Farsalinos, Romagna, Allifranchini, et al., 2013). It is pertinent to note that e-cigarette vapor is significantly less cytotoxic than cigarette smoke (Romagna et al., 2013; Farsalinos, Romagna, Allifranchini, et al., 2013; Misra et al., 2014). It was suggested that concern over repeated inhalation of the vapor was not borne out of toxicity studies and that the risk of accidental poisoning was no different from other widely available household chemicals (Wagener et al., 2012). Indeed, a more recent study reported no meaningful toxic effects, that is no induction of cytotoxic, genotoxic or inflammatory effects, with e-cigarette use (Misra et al., 2014).

An appraisal of potential risks of e-cigarettes compared with the well-established harms of smoking tobacco cigarettes outlined chemical toxicology, passive vaping, and adolescent use (Farsalinos & Polosa, 2014). E-cigarette emissions were found to contain ultrafine particulate matter formed from supersaturated vapor (Pellegrino et al., 2012; Schober et al., 2014). Secondhand e-cigarette emissions may involuntarily expose non-users to nicotine, but not toxic tobacco-specific combustion byproducts (Czogala et al., 2013; Goniewicz et al., 2014) and poses no apparent risk to human health (McAuley et al., 2012). It was suggested that there would be an increase in accidental exposure to e-cigarette fluids at poison centers, although such incidents are unlikely to result in serious toxicity (Cantrell, 2014). It has been found that high voltage e-cigarettes may expose users to carbonyl compounds (Kosmider et al., 2014). Short-term pulmonary effects of respiratory flow resistance and impedance as well as exhaled nitric oxide have been reported (Vardavas et al., 2012). Risk of passive nicotine exposure (Ballbè et al., 2014) and passive vaping (Schripp et al., 2013) is to be expected from the consumption of e-cigarettes and consequent effect on airways due to vapor, nicotine content, and particle dose received (Marini et al., 2014). The risk of passive smoking exposure from e-cigarettes was modest due to half-life of the vapor in air of 11 seconds before evaporating compared to 19-20 minutes of smoke dissipating (Bertholon et al., 2013); nonetheless, e-cigarettes generate smaller change in lung function similar to the nicotinergic impact of cigarettes (Flouris et al., 2013). The concern that e-cigarettes promote continued smoking by enabling smokers to cope with no-smoking environments was countered by the observation that most smokers use the devices in order to quit and that this use appears to enhance the motivation for the same (Wagener et al., 2012). In addition, e-cigarettes used in no-smoking areas posed no discernible risk to bystanders (Nitzkin, 2014). It was further observed that e-cigarettes may reduce toxin exposure to non-smokers compared to cigarettes (Wagener et al., 2012). E-cigarette use did not discourage, and may encourage, cigarette or dual use among adolescents (Camenga et al., 2014; Dutra & Glantz, 2014; Lee, Grana & Glantz, 2014). Contrary to these reports, it was found that e-cigarettes have not been attractive to non-smoking teens and adults, i.e. limited numbers have experimented but hardly any continued use (Nitzkin, 2014). No evidence of regular e-cigarette use by never-smokers or by non-smoking children (Hajek et al., 2014) and very little evidence of use among adults who have never smoked (Dockrell et al., 2013). Because of many methodological issues, severe conflicts of interest, inconsistent contradictory results, and lack of long-term follow-up, it is difficult to conclude the health consequences of e-cigarette use (Pisinger & Døssing, 2014).

Health outcomes were more clearly delineated. E-cigarette use was perceived as a healthier and more acceptable alternative to smoking cigarettes (van Staden et al., 2013). The vast majority of e-cigarette use was by former smokers using them to avoid relapse, alleviate withdrawal symptoms, and to reduce cigarette consumption or to quit (Etter & Bullen, 2011a; Dawkins et al., 2012; Goniewicz, Lingas & Hajek, 2013; Nitzkin, 2014), even among smokers not intending to quit (Nides et al., 2014; Polosa et al., 2011; Polosa, Caponnetto, et al., 2014). During use of e-cigarettes, the daily cigarette consumption of smokers decreased significantly (Miura et al., 2011). Indeed, daily use of e-cigarettes for at least one month was strongly associated with quitting smoking at two to three years follow-up (Biener & Hargraves, 2014).

Reduction of tobacco-related withdrawal symptoms and urge to smoke were reported after e-cigarette use as well (Dawkins & Corcoran, 2014). Increased duration of e-cigarette use was associated with smoking fewer cigarettes per day (Lechner et al., 2014). The use of e-cigarettes to substitute smoking also lead to reduced cigarette consumption with subsequent improvements in asthmatic symptoms (Polosa, Morjaria, Caponnetto, Caruso, et al., 2014). E-cigarette users also tended to decrease nicotine content (Lechner et al., 2014). Most former smokers expressed concern that they might relapse to smoking if they stopped e-cigarette use (Etter & Bullen, 2011a).

Laboratory findings have indicated that e-cigarettes deliver clinically significant doses of nicotine and reduce abstinence symptoms with lower potential for abuse relative to cigarettes (Vansickel, Weaver, & Eissenberg, 2012). Nicotine levels appeared to play a role in achieving and maintaining smoking cessation (Farsalinos, Romagna, Tsiapras, et al., 2013). E-cigarettes as a NRT appeared to be immediately and highly effective in reducing craving and withdrawal symptoms (Adriaens et al., 2014). E-cigarettes were found to contribute to relapse prevention in former smokers and smoking cessation in current smokers including those with recurring relapses (Caponnetto, Polosa et al, 2011; Etter & Bullen, 2014). Among smokers who attempted to stop without professional support, e-cigarette users were more likely to report continued abstinence than those who used over-the-counter NRTs or no cessation aids (Brown et al., 2014). E-cigarettes hold promise as a smoking cessation method (Siegel, Tanwar, & Wood, 2011). Long-term e-cigarette use, with or without nicotine, was shown to substantially decrease cigarette consumption in smokers not willing to quit and was well tolerated, eliciting enduring tobacco abstinence (Caponnetto et al., 2013; Polosa, Morjaria, Caponnetto, Campagna, et al., 2014). Nicotine-free inhalators have been beneficial in the context of smoking cessation as an intervention addressing the behavioral component of smoking addiction (Caponnetto, Cibella et al., 2011), and e-cigarettes can be used in this fashion. E-cigarettes were found to be efficacious tools for addressing the impact of behavioral and social components of smoking addiction (Barbeau, Burda & Siegel, 2013).

These devices appear to increase motivation to quit, curb abstinence-induced craving and withdrawal symptoms during a quit attempt, and promote abstinence maintenance. These characteristics afford e-cigarettes strong potential as a cessation tool in the context of harm reduction. An analysis of e-cigarette users' health behavior in this context may inform future use of these devices as a structured intervention for smoking cessation.

Personality

Motivation to quit has been attributed to several factors, including readiness to change, expectations for support, and the costs and benefits of behavior change (Manfredi et al., 1998). Personality structure plays a role in an individual's ability to successfully undertake the health behavior of smoking cessation. Understanding these personality dynamics will enable improved efficacy in treatment. From a review of the book, subsequently supplied, certain personality factors involved in resiliency to addiction have emerged. These include traits of Self-Efficacy, Hardiness, and Grit, among others.

Purpose Statement

The purpose of this study was to determine personality factor correlates of smoking cessation efficacy among e-cigarette users.

Research Questions

1. Do identified personality factors impact smoking cessation efficacy among e-cigarette users?

2. Is there a particular personality structure associated with successful smoking cessation?
3. Are there personality factors that best predict the success of self-assisted quit attempts using e-cigarettes?

Application of Results

An understanding of underlying personality structures related to the use of e-cigarettes in smoking cessation will inform the debate on the clinical utility of the use of the devices as well as collateral use in treatment programs. In a broader context, an understanding of psychological dynamics involved in self-assisted smoking cessation will contribute to a better understanding of the adoption of health behaviors, which in turn will be applicable to the development of treatment techniques for both chemical use and compulsive behavior. Furthermore, within the context of the public health issue of smoking, data concerning e-cigarette use toward cessation will be useful in formulating public policy with regard to control and regulation.

Theoretical Framework

Smoking was conceptualized as an addiction according to DSM 5 (APA, 2013) criteria for substance-related disorders. This conceptualization integrates both physiological addiction to the chemical nicotine and behavioral addiction to smoking rituals. It represents the most current psychodiagnostic definition of tobacco cigarette addiction and engages the complete role that substitution with e-cigarettes plays for a user, not only as a nicotine delivery device but also as a proxy for cigarette manipulation, smoke inhalation, and other behaviors that characterize use.

The process of smoking cessation has been delineated along the lines of the Transtheoretical Model Stages of Change. In this model intention and behavior are measured according to the following five stages of change: precontemplation, in which there is no intention to change in the next 6 months; contemplation, in which there is an intention to take action in the same time; preparation, in which there is intention to change behavior within one month; action, the stage in which a new behavior has been adopted and maintained for less than 6 months; and the maintenance stage, in which the behavior has been maintained for more than 6 months (Prochaska, Redding, & Evers, 2002). Metricizing cessation in these terms suggests that although precursors take place in preparation quit attempts occur during action and continue in maintenance, as the names imply; therefore, successful smoking cessation was conceptualized as abstinence for more than 6 months. It is pertinent to note that not all e-cigarette users smoke tobacco cigarettes or use e-cigarettes for the purpose of smoking cessation; however, these users represent a pattern of use outside the scope of the study and were not investigated.

Definitions

E-cigarette: Any of a number of battery-operated devices that vaporizes fluid with or without nicotine to simulate a cigarette.

E-cigarette user: An individual who uses e-cigarettes alone or concurrently with tobacco cigarettes.

Smoking: Use of tobacco cigarettes.

Smoking cessation: The health behavior of abstinence from smoking, with successful cessation lasting at least 6 months.

Outline of Remaining Chapters

Chapter 2 will review the related book concerning personality factors involved in health protective behaviors. The research design and methodology of the present study will be presented in Chapter 3. Study findings and an analysis of the data collected will follow in Chapter 4. Finally, Chapter 5 will encompass a summary of the study, a discussion of the implications, and recommendations for treatment planning as well as future research.

Chapter 2:
Review of Related Book

Chapter Overview

This chapter will review historical and recent book on health behavior and personality correlates. It will detail personality factors that have emerged as important to the adoption of health behaviors, including Grit, Self-Efficacy, Hardiness, Conscientiousness and Neuroticism.

The present study is intended to fill a gap in the book on the health behavior harm reduction as it relates to smoking cessation. The focus on e-cigarettes parallels a recent trend among smokers attempting to quit (Caponnetto, Polosa et al, 2011; Etter & Bullen, 2011a; Miura et al., 2011; Polosa et al., 2011; Siegel et al., 2011; Dawkins et al., 2012; Vansickel et al., 2012; Wagener et al., 2012; Barbeau et al., 2013; Caponnetto et al., 2013; Goniewicz, Lingas, et al., 2013; King et al., 2013; van Staden et al., 2013; Adriaens et al., 2014; Biener & Hargraves, 2014; Brown et al., 2014; Dawkins & Corcoran, 2014; Etter & Bullen, 2014; Farsalinos, Romagna, et al., 2014; Hajek et al., 2014; Lechner et al., 2014; Nides et al., 2014; Nitzkin, 2014; Polosa, Caponnetto, et al., 2014; Polosa, Morjaria, Caponnetto, Campagna, et al., 2014) and addresses a gap in the book on the clinical utility of e-cigarettes as it pertains to the effectiveness as an addiction treatment.

Importance of the Topic

The formulation of a comprehensive personality profile of successful smoking cessation has not previously been explored. By developing an aggregate profile of individuals who successfully quit with a self-assisted attempt, enables better treatment planning for treating recidivism and individuals unwilling or unable to quit. The clinical utility of this research is in developing treatment programs.

There is also regulatory utility in determining the psychological correlates of smoking cessation by way of e-cigarette in so far as informing debate on public policy. Determining whether or not e-cigarette use is measurably related to individuals' affinity to resiliency in addiction offers support or opposition for regulatory measures. It also affords ability to improve treatment approaches and thereby holds value in developing policy consistent with positive health outcomes.

Review of Historical Background

A review of the history of psychological research on the role of personality factors in health behavior follows. The pertinent line of research concerns the motivation to engage in health behavior. This line of research has utility particularly with respect to resiliency in addiction. An emergent construct was locus of control, which predicated research on the identification of specific personality factors conducive to health protective behavior.

Personality Constructs Related to Health Behavior

Brousseau and Mallinger (1981) examined the relationship between internal-external locus of control and perceived occupational stress as related to cardiovascular health. Previous research had elucidated locus of control as an influence on stress reactions, primarily that beliefs about an internal locus of control were associated with experiencing less stress than those of an external locus of control. It was hypothesized that external locus of control would correlate positively with both cardiovascular ill health and occupational stress, which in turn were hypothesized to correlate positively with each other. The research also sought to measure the change in magnitude between correlations of external locus of control and cardiovascular ill health after statistically controlling perceived occupational stress, the assumption being that there would be a decrease due to the influence of locus of control on perceived stress and therefore upon health.

The study was conducted utilizing a sample of 101 dentists attending a California Dental Association meeting in 1978 who had requested a cardiovascular health examination at the time, with the inclusion criteria being those with blood pressure readings less than one standard deviation below the age-adjusted national mean in order to examine variations from normalcy to hypertension or high-blood-pressure. The Locus of Control Scale (Rotter, 1966) was utilized for measuring locus of control, perceived occupational stress was calculated by summing responses to nine six-point Likert scale items developed from previous research indicating that problems encountered in dealing with patients are perceived by dentists as a major source of stress, and cardiovascular health was measured by systolic blood pressure, diastolic blood pressure, and by electrocardiogram.

The cardiovascular health of the sample was overall favorable, with only nine dentists receiving abnormal readings; however, of the hypotheses predicted, only a positive correlation between external locus of control and cardiovascular ill health was found. Perceived stress failed to correlate with locus of control or any cardiovascular health indices; therefore, controlling for perceived stress returned negligible results with respect to the magnitude of relational changes.

The research identified support for the notion that cardiovascular health is related to beliefs about external locus of control, but not stress perceptions. An explanation was considered that those with greater internal locus of control, those believing themselves capable of influencing their circumstances and actively seeking means of reducing or eliminating stressors, may experience less psychological and physiological distress. The implication for future research was that perceptions of stress may be less important in the long run than how individuals behave when confronted with difficult situations.

Kobasa, Maddi, and Kahn (1982) sought to answer the question of what particular personality dispositions mitigate the effects of stressful life events. A study was designed to test whether or not the hypobook that the personality predisposition of Hardiness- commitment, control, and challenge- functioned to decrease the effect of stress in producing illness symptoms. The investigation was nested in the body of research examining the relationship between stress and illness, and further on the cusp of a shift toward so-called resistance resources assisting individuals overcome stressful life events, which marked a change in focus on personality characteristics, for example, resilience, Self-Efficacy, and Hardiness.

The study surveyed upper-level managers (*n*=670) of a large utility company with questionnaires integrating measures of stressful life events via an adaptation of the Schedule of Life Events and symptomatology via the Seriousness of Illness Survey as well as measures of personality dispositions of commitment, control, and challenge each by two scales, i.e. respectively, the Alienation From Self and Alienation From Work subscales of the Alienation Test; the External Locus of Control Scale as well as the Powerlessness Scale of the Alienation Test; and the Security Scale of the California Life Goals Evaluation Schedule in addition to the Cognitive Structure Scale of the Personality Research Form.

The results of this investigation supported the hypobook that Hardiness decreased the effect of stressful life events in producing illness symptoms. The significant main effect due to Hardiness in the analyses of covariance suggested that the tendency toward commitment, control, and challenge functioned as a resistance resource; however, the concurrent estimate of stressful life events' relationship to illness increase was mitigated by a weaker trend that did not reach conventional significance levels of prospective estimates of the same.

The implications of the research were twofold. First, that a personality construct of stress resistance could be measurably linked to health form the basis of the present research on the health behavior of smoking cessation and its relationship to personality constructs. Second, the doubts of a causal link of personality factors influencing health status suggest that stress resistance may not represent a complete outline of the personality dynamics in overcoming health problems. The study provided a future direction of examining interactions among resistance resources.

Seeman and Seeman (1983) investigated the relationship between a sense of control and the significance for health. Re-examining locus of control research which had drawn attention to the tendency of an internal locus of control, that is the belief in the efficacy of one's actions, being related to a greater likelihood of engaging in health-promoting behavior was intended to enrich the book through a longitudinal study of a large, representative sample with a broader range of health indices. Three domains of health behavior were identified, as follows: utilization of preventative care, health knowledge, and exhibiting the physical status of healthy behavior, i.e. absence of acute and chronic illness. Essentially an *a priori* prediction, a greater sense of control was hypothesized to be reflected in the three domains.

The method that was employed was a three-stage random probability sample of panel interviews in Los Angeles County with sampling units based on census tracts, racial-ethnic composition, and divergent demographic characteristics. The sample consisted of 1,210 adults in initial telephone interviews with six-week call-backs at six week intervals, of which 931 participants were re-interviewed during the study year later in a final face-to-face interview. Initial interviews contained questions about health beliefs, while final interviews contained questions concerning knowledge about cancer. Neither initial nor final interviews contained the questions regarding control, the independent variable, which were posed at after the interval before the conclusion of the study. The procedure called for participants to be queried initially about health problems, and the call-back designed to control those who reported illness initially. These respondents who were initially ill were then called back and asked detailed questions about their illness in order to obtain sense-of-health-control responses after the first call-back in which no illness had occurred during the preceding six to eight weeks, while respondents who were initially without illness answered the same eleven-item health locus of control scale at the first follow-up. In this fashion 87% (*n*=1,054) participants provided health control scores over the course of seven call-backs. The scale which was utilized was developed by Wallston and included fatalistic (external) and control-oriented (internal) items rated on a four-point agree or disagree scale.

A sense of low control was found to be significantly associated with less self-initiated preventative care, less optimism concerning the efficacy of early treatment, poorer self-rated health, as well as more episodes of illness, more bed confinements, and greater dependence on physicians. A poignant finding related to the present research was identified in the domain of preventative health behaviors as related to cigarette smoking. Sense of control as defined by a luck denial scale was evident among indifferent smokers, those having made no effort to quit, who scored higher in external locus of control than compared to concerned respondents who had taken some health-conscious action, that is, nonsmokers, those who had succeeded in quitting, and recidivists who had tried unsuccessfully to quit. The perceived degree of threat associated with smoking additionally played a predictable role. When cancer risk was perceived as greater the expectancy for control was not significant, but when threat was perceived to be ambiguous the sense of control played a more prominent role in the difference between indifferent smokers and the concerned group. It was suggested that in the case of smoking high threat overrode expectancy for control, while lower perceived threat revealed a significantly more external health orientation among indifferent smokers.

The research demonstrated a link between positive health behaviors and a sense of control. The implication as it pertains to the use of e-cigarettes in cessation is that the greater control over nicotine consumption afforded by variable content in e-cigarette fluid may support harm reduction. The health behavior of cessation was associated with this sense of control.

Review of Current Research Book

Five Factor Traits

Bermúdez (1999) outlined that the study of health problems has focused on the psychosocial factors related to the development of health problems and less so on the mechanisms explaining the persistence of adverse risky behaviors over those increasing quality of life. Research that has investigated these mechanisms was delineated into two lines. The first deals with predisposition to patterns of behavior and the second the processes that explain how behaviors are initiated, maintained, or changed.

Predisposition has been measured according to a variable approach. It was suggested that this approach enables the assessment of individual vulnerabilities as well as the variables where focus may improve individual health. Correlational studies were found to have identified the variables of Conscientiousness, Hardiness, and Self-Efficacy among others as positively associated with health behavior as well as a negative association of Neuroticism. In particular, the emergence of a consensus was found on the use of the Five Factor Model- which consists of the broad dimensions Openness, Conscientiousness, Extraversion, Agreeableness, and Neuroticism that incorporate research results generated from other models (Costa & McCrae, 1992)- as a framework for research on personality and health behavior.

The research focused on the processes was summarized as sharing a common general hypobook of behavior being rational and intentional. Numerous, well-supported models have been advanced, prominently the Health Belief Model, Protection Motivation Theory, Precaution Adoption Process, Theory of Reasoned Action, Theory of Planned Behavior, Subjective Expected Utility Theory, and the Comprehensive Health Seeking and Coping Paradigm. Models such as these serve as heuristics for the design of intervention programs.

With respect to smoking harm reduction, the overall process might be conceptualized clearly in terms of quitting as benchmarked previously according to the Transtheoretical Model of Change, although the motivational processes underlying change warrant further study elsewhere. The process involved in the health behavior of adopting the e-cigarette alternative to smoking is the focus of the current investigation. Whether or not there are dispositional differences in cessation efficacy among e-cigarette users will elucidate its value as an intervention, either structured or self-assisted. Developing this basis will enable future understanding of the psychological processes, of which many frameworks already exist for other NRTs.

Judge et al. (2002) identified an interesting concept with regard to self-esteem, locus of control, and Neuroticism as well as the closely-related trait of generalized Self-Efficacy. It was hypothesized that these measures share a common core construct. Meta-analytic findings were found revealing a strong relationship across the traits explainable by a second-order latent factor. That these traits were not entirely independent of each other was supported by discriminant validity among measures in heteromethod-heterotrait correlations, but not monomethod-heterotrait correlations. It was also supported by the emergence of consistent patterns of correlations. It was suggested that rather than abandon the constructs all together, that an integration of the variance from unique aspects of each be explored perhaps as indicators of a core construct similar to although more more broadly defined than Neuroticism. However, it was further stipulated that these traits cannot be subsumed under Neuroticism due to somewhat stronger correlations with other Five Factor traits. As it applies to present research, this concept has utility in elucidating a progression of different trait characteristics along process lines of the development of cessation.

One poignant process was described by Koelen and Lindström (2005), the principle of empowerment. A widely used definition of empowerment is the sense of control over one's personality, cognition, and motivation. Two concepts were identified in this salutogenic perspective on health generation, those of general resistance resources and sense of coherence, the ability to use such resources. The influence of these empowerment factors were conceptualized as a means of changing in the direction of positive health. Empowerment was related to similar concepts of Resilience, the ability to cope successfully in the face of adversity or risk (Werner & Smith, 1982), and Hardiness, the combination of the following three elements: control, the tendency to believe and act as if one can influence outcomes; commitment, the ability to believe in the importance of one's actions; and challenge, the belief in a norm of change rather than stability (Kobasa, 1982). It was suggested that the synbook of these concepts afford a clearer definition of empowerment as the process of mastery over one's life in which a closer correspondence between goals and a sense of how to achieve them is gained as well as the relationship between efforts and outcomes.

The factors that influence psychological empowerment were identified as locus of control, learned helplessness, Self-Efficacy, and outcome expectations. As relevant to cessation efficacy afforded by e-cigarettes, each factor may be conceptualized as having a particular role. Locus of control can be conceptualized as the choice to use the device. Learned helplessness, a lowered state of functioning rooted in uncontrollability (Seligman, 1975), can be likened to smoking addiction. Self-Efficacy, the belief in one's capability to organize and execute courses of action required by prospective situations (Bandura, 1977), might directly refer to the device usage coupled with graduated decrease of nicotine content as has been previously observed characteristic of e-cigarette users (Lechner et al., 2014). And expected outcome, not surprisingly, reflects harm reduction and ultimately cessation. It appears that e-cigarette use is amenable to empowering smokers to make self-assisted quit attempts. Evidence also supports positive outcomes of this method.

Self-Efficacy

Self-Efficacy in promoting the health behavior of smoking cessation was examined in further detail by Gulzar et al. (2009). Self-Efficacy plays a role in transforming behavior at an attitudinal level. That is, possessing Self-Efficacy by believing that one is able to achieve a desired goal enables behavior change. It was described as motivating and directing an individual, the efforts, flexibility, and consistency to perform challenging tasks as well as influencing the performance of accomplishments. Learning experiences were considered a major determinant of efficacy expectations, experiences of mastery instilled confidence influencing positive Self-Efficacy while experiences of failure influences negatively. It was explained that empowerment emerges from Self-Efficacy and impacts decision-making and generates sustainable health-promoting behavior. E.g. a smoker who successfully quits smoking might then plan to reduce weight; the past success of health modification motivates new activities, a sense of accomplishment, and health promotion.

Dickens, Staniford, and Long (2013) conducted a study to investigate smoking behavior, motivations, and Self-Efficacy among patients and staff at a psychiatric hospital. Because people with mental disorders account for a disproportionate percentage of smokers, comparative data with a normative population provided by the staff respondents was expected to elicit rich data. A self-report questionnaire was designed to assess nicotine dependence by the Fagerström Test for Nicotine Dependence, craving, cessation attempts, motives for smoking using the Smoker Clinic Questionnaire, motivation to quit smoking via the 10-point Contemplation Ladder and a single item "Would you like to stop smoking?" as well as the Reasons for Quitting Questionnaire, and Self-Efficacy with a single item "On a scale of 1 to 10 where 1 is not at all confident and 10 I extremely confident, how confident are you that you can quit smoking now?"

Of the 100 recruited respondents, half were patients and half staff. Patients were assessed at significantly higher levels of dependence and craving. Patients reported an average of 1 quit attempt over the past year and rated lower Self-Efficacy; however, these scores were not significantly different from staff scores. Staff indicated higher levels of motivation to quit.

Patient were more likely to give coping as a motivation to smoke as well as to be motivated by both boredom and pleasure. The lack of significant differences suggested that Self-Efficacy alone is not a highly discriminating variable, or at least in the context of the limitations of the settings. Indeed both groups responded at about the same level of Self-Efficacy, indicative of the stage of change of precontemplation or contemplation. In addition, it appeared that a greater concern with health consequences as a motivation to quit did not in turn motivate quit attempts, at least in this limited setting. The implication for examining Self-Efficacy among e-cigarette users is that other personality factors should be considered also. It is also likely that individuals already engaging in a behavior change may have higher Self-Efficacy ratings than smokers not engaged in a quit attempt or perhaps this lack of Self-Efficacy variation was an effect generated by the assessment metric of a single item.

Hardiness

Brooks (2003) examined the relationship between health-related Hardiness and chronic illness. The tendency of chronic illness, an altered health state that cannot be cured by a medical procedure, to compound serious health issues prompted an examination of Hardiness in order to identify practice implications. A meta-analysis of research between 1966 and 2002 was conducted on the Pub-Med, Medline, CINAHL databases. Populations of interest were adults with hemophilia and either hepatitis C virus (HCV) or human immunodeficiency virus (HIV) or both. Search terms were as follows: adaptation, chronic illness, HCV, health-related hardines, hemophilia, HIV. Articles were excluded if they were not abstract, not written in English, or subjects did not have chronic illness. Two additional studies were included because of importance to the review. Based on these inclusion/exclusion criteria, 107 articles were reviewed.

Patients were found to encounter demands of the cost of care and insurance, stigmatism, fear of bloodborne pathogens, drug shortages, negotiating home care, and interacting with the healthcare system. It was suggested that stress-resistance such as through hardiness had potential to moderate these demands by incorporating lifestyle changes. The belief of hardy people of their own ability to influence life events rather than to be helpless, that is active involvement rather than passivity or alienation, were found to improve psychosocial adaptation.

Abdollahi and Talib (2014) conducted a study to examine the associations between Hardiness, problem-solving skills, and attitudes towards cigarette smoking among adolescents. It was reported that hardy individuals appraise stressful conditions as more challenging and controllable as well as less threatening, and that these individuals were more likely to gain experience from such events. Hardiness theory was cited as having outlined that high-hardy individuals were more optimistic, flexible, and likely to use adaptive coping styles than the low-hardy, also more likely to report happiness, life satisfaction, and mental and physical health. Although perceived stress had been identified as an important factor in adolescent substance use, no research existed on relationships between smoking and Hardiness. The study aimed to address this gap in research.

It was hypothesized that Hardiness and poor problem-solving skills appraisal would be negatively associated with a positive attitude toward smoking. To test this hypobook, 550 male high school students aged 16 to 19 years were recruited and administered a questionnaire. The questionnaire consisted of the Personal Views Survey, Problem-Solving Inventory, and the Attitude towards Smoking Scale. The survey data was submitted to Structural Equation Modeling analysis.

The results indicated that Hardiness and problem-solving skills were predictors of negative attitudes toward cigarette smoking, supporting previous research. The findings also improved this research in two ways. First, the analysis revealed Hardiness was a protective factor against smoking. It was asserted that high-hardy adolescents may have better strategies for solving problems and therefore may perceive risky behavior as a less effective social strategy. Second, the research identified that problem-solving skills were also a protective factor against smoking. It was found that because individuals, especially adolescents, may adopt smoking as a solution to stressful life events or a solution to daily stressors, developed problem-solving skills serve as a psychological protective factor against smoking.

These conclusions suggest that the health behavior of smoking cessation may likewise be positively correlated with Hardiness among smokers. Individuals who have adopted the behavior may exercise the same psychological dynamics in affecting change to that same behavior toward a healthier lifestyle. Thus, the successful use of e-cigarettes in the context of smoking cessation are expected to also be associated with high Hardiness.

Grit

The personality trait Grit has been defined as perseverance and passion for long-term goals, which entails strenuously working toward challenges by maintaining both effort and interest despite adversity in progress; furthermore, Grit differs from Self-Efficacy beliefs about ability to succeed by tapping long-term stamina or persistence and shows predictive validity over the closely-related trait Conscientiousness which does not include the element of long-term persistence (Duckworth et al., 2007). Grit has been examined in a variety of contexts. Reed, Pritschet and Cutton (2013) researched Grit and Conscientiousness for the health behavior of exercise. A study was designed to investigate psychological variables Grit and Conscientiousness as related to Transtheoretical Models stage of change position for exercise participation. Hypotheses were laid out that there would be a positive association between Grit, Conscientiousness, and stages of change as well as that Grit would perform equivalently or better than Conscientiousness in predicting exercise stage of change level.

Participants were recruited from students, staff, and faculty at three universities yielding 1,171 survey responses. The survey consisted of a stage of change measure with respect to exercise relative to frequency and duration per week, the Short Grit Scale, and the Big Five Inventory Conscientiousness dimension. The stage of change measure was delineated low, moderate, or high intensity staging questions which read as "Do you exercise at a [intensity level] intensity at least three times per week for more than 15 minutes?" with five response choices as follows: Yes, I have been exercising at a [intensity] for more than six months (maintenance); Yes, I have been exercising at a [intensity] for less than six months (action); No, but I plan to start exercising at a [intensity] in the next 30 days (preparaton); No, but I plan to start exercising at a [intensity] in the next six months (contemplation); or, No, and I don't plan to start exercising at a [intensity] in the next six months (precontemplation). The Short Grit Scale consists of eight items rated on a five-point scale from 1 = not at all like me to 5 = very much like me and a measure of Grit is obtained by averaging all responses. The Conscientiousness measure was composed of the sentence “I see myself as someone who...” followed by short phrases based on prototypical adjectives associated with the trait rated from 1 = disagree strongly to 5 = agree strongly.

The survey was administered online requiring five to seven minutes to complete and remained available for three weeks. Data analysis was conducted utilizing SPSS software. Prior to data analysis, the database of responses was screened for validation and six cases removed due to outlying or missing values. An analysis of variance was conducted in order to validate stage of change. It was found that Grit and Conscientiousness were positively correlated with exercise stage of change, although neither variable was related to to low intensity stage of change. This result suggested that these constructs were not crucial for the initiation of the health behavior, but were important higher stages of change. It was further demonstrated that Grit outperformed Conscientiousness in predicting the stage of change perhaps due to exercise regimen often involving progression to higher intensity as fitness improves and requires persistence month after month to attain higher fitness levels.

As it relates to the study of health behavior, Grit represents a trait warranting further research in other health behavior areas. In addition, the framework of Transtheoretical Model of change represents a valuable method to understand the process of behavior change. Grit may prove to be a better predictor of behavior change than other identified personality factors.

Maddi et al. (2013) conducted a study of the relative effectiveness of the protective factors Hardiness, Grit, and emotional intelligence on the negative performance considerations of internet addiction, excessive consumer spending, and gambling. A survey was designed and administered to 425 undergraduates at a public university. It consisted of the Personal View Survey, the 12-item Grit Scale, Emotional Intelligence Scale, Revised and performance variables. The performance variables included the Canadian Problem Gambling Index, a measure of monetary conservation drawn from items on the Money Ethic Scale as well as two measures of excessive consumer spending by way of the Money Attitude Scale and the Compulsive Buying Scale, and additionally a measure of internet addiction from the Problem Internet Usage Survey.

The analysis of survey results revealed overall patterns of intercorrelations between dispositional variables and multiple regression analyses the effectiveness of the personality measures on the dependent performance measures. In this fashion, shared variance among personality constructs was eliminated in order to identify particular contributions to the performance variables. None of the three personality variables were significant predictors of gambling measures according to the regression analysis; however, relationships were found with respect to the other performance variables. A positive relationship was found between emotional intelligence and monetary conservation. Hardiness was negatively related to excessive consumer spending. Both Grit and Hardiness were negative predictors of internet addiction, Hardiness the stronger of the two.

A possible explanation for the better prediction of protection against internet addiction associated with Hardiness over Grit was suggested in that while both afford ability to deal with ongoing stressors, the characteristic existential courage of Hardiness allows evaluation, effort to resolve, and growth through the process of dealing with stressors may be more efficacious than the predefined goal-orientation of Grit irrespective of the stressful circumstance. Regarding excessive consumer spending, it was found that the stronger the Hardiness level, the less likelihood of overspending on unneeded items, just compulsively, or for fun; furthermore, the lack of predictive validity with Grit could be explained as with the previous performance variable. Monetary conservation was only related to emotional intelligence in the regression analysis possibly due to the sample representing a population already overlooking monetary conservation in order to succeed in undergraduate education; therefore, the positive correlations with Hardiness and Grit may not have persisted in the regression analysis. In the same way, gambling had no statistically significant relationships in the regression analysis due to an apparent small percentage of undergraduates being gamblers. Only 57 respondents completed the gambling test which had instructions to skip if the individual was not a gambler.

Nonetheless, compulsive behavior was negatively correlated with both Hardiness and Grit. Pertaining to smoking cessation, there is an element of compulsive behavior involved in the ritual and behavioral element of smoking. Hardiness as well as Grit thus represent useful personality traits for examining the health behavior of e-cigarette use among smokers.

Evaluation of Research Book

Early psychological research identified a sense of control as an important factor in the adoption and longevity of health behaviors. E-cigarettes provide a sense of control over not only the use of nicotine via varying concentrations in vaporizing fluids, but by providing an alternative to emulate the act of smoking and thereby the rituals associated with use. These characteristics afford e-cigarettes a unique position among NRTs. The characteristic of reducing harm in virtually every respect further increase sense of control over the health behavior.

A major contemporary model of personality, the Five Factor Model, has been related to health behavior. In particular, Conscientiousness is positively correlated while Neuroticism is negatively correlated. These global factors have in turn been related to other factors that emerged as prominently researched factors related to health behaviors, including Self-Efficacy, Hardiness, and Grit. It has been suggested that these personality factors overlap to some extent, and that each encompasses unique facets of similar domains. Table 1 lists the definitions and relation to health behaviors for each of these identified personality factors.

Overall the identified personality factors seem to support cessation efficacy, with the exception of Neuroticism which may be expected to counteract cessation efficacy. The role personality factors play in the successful use of e-cigarettes for smoking cessation has not previously been studied. Understanding what effect, if any, self-control of Conscientiousness or lack thereof of Neuroticism, self-belief of Self-Efficacy, stress resistance of Hardiness, and goal-orientation of Grit have on the successful reduction of harm and smoking cessation will improve clinical treatments; furthermore, delineating these effects in terms of progress along the process of cessation will lead to more effective interventions for smoking.

It is hypothesized that global traits of neuroticism and conscientiousness will mediate cessation efficacy along with nicotine dependence. High levels of neuroticism and nicotine dependence will limit an e-cigarette user's ability to initiate abstinence, while a high degree of conscientiousness will promote initial abstinence. It is further expected that self-efficacy will play a role in early stages of change, specifically in precontemplation and contemplation stages. Hardiness will, in turn, support the action stage in which an e-cigarette user initiates abstinence. And finally it is anticipated that Grit will be positively associated with maintaining the e-cigarette replacement of tobacco cigarettes. The present study evaluated these hypotheses of personality traits (see Table 1) related to health behavior impacting cessation efficacy of e-cigarette use.

Table 1

Definitions of Identified Personality Factors

Trait	Definition	Relation to Health Behavior
Conscientiousness	The tendency to be planful, organized, and carry out tasks; purposeful, strong-willed, and determined (Costa & McCrae, 1992).	Self-control and the ability to resist impulses and temptations is associated with achievement (Costa & McCrae, 1992).
Neuroticism	The tendency to experience negative affects; susceptibility to psychological distress (Costa & McCrae, 1992)	Susceptibility to disruptive emotions interferes with adaptation, impulse control, and ability to cope with stress (Costa & McCrae, 1992).
Self-Efficacy	The confidence an individual has in the ability to perform a novel or difficult task, or cope with adversity (Schwarzer, 1992).	Perceived self-efficacy facilitates goal-setting, effort investment, persistence in face of barriers and recovery from setbacks (Schwarzer, 1992).
Hardiness	General dispositions of commitment, control, and challenge that function as a stress resistance resource (Kobasa, 1979).	Hardy individuals appraise stressful conditions as more controllable, less threatening, and are more likely to gain experience from them (Abdollahi & Talib, 2014).
Grit	The tendency to work toward challenges by maintaining both effort and interest despite adversity in progress; perseverance and passion for long-term goals (Duckworth et al., 2007).	Gritty individuals possess the ability to succeed in their goals by tapping long-term stamina and persistence (Duckworth et al., 2007).

Summary

A dearth of current studies on personality factors related to the efficacy of e-cigarette use in smoking cessation warrant the application of established smoking-related health behavior research to this area of study. A number of personality factors are applicable to e-cigarette use in the context of a health behavior. The results of the present study will benefit clinical treatment as well as inform public health policy. E-cigarettes may afford considerable impact on reducing tobacco-related harm in communities and investigating its practical treatment value will increase this potential.

Chapter 3: Research Design and Method

Chapter Overview

In order to examine the relationships of personality factors to the stage of change during the health behavior of smoking cessation via adoption of e-cigarettes, a one-time survey was administered. The research design followed a variable approach with independent variables of Self-Efficacy, Hardiness, Grit, Neuroticism and Conscientiousness measured by various instruments as well as prior nicotine dependence and stage of change measured by duration of e-cigarette use analyzed against dependent variables of nicotine content, tobacco and e-cigarette use. It was expected that each of the personality factors would correlate positively with successful cessation, except for Neuroticism which would correlate negatively; that higher nicotine dependence would be associated with higher Neuroticism and be correlated with continued smoking during the cessation attempt representing a preparatory stage of change.

Purpose Statement

The purpose of this study was to determine personality factor correlates of smoking cessation efficacy among e-cigarette users.

Hypotheses and Rationales

Several hypotheses were tested for significance at an alpha level of 0.05. The test which was used to assess nicotine dependence was the Fagerström Test for Nicotine Dependence (FTND). The tests utilized to assess personality factors consisted of appropriate scales from psychometrically strong instruments as follows: for Self-Efficacy, the Generalized Self-Efficacy Scale (GSE); Neuroticism and Conscientiousness, the corresponding subscales of the NEO Five Factor Inventory (NEO-FFI-3); Hardiness, the Dispositional Resilience Scale (DRS-II); and Grit, the Short Grit Scale (Grit-S). Patterns of use were assessed by the survey designed by

Goniewicz, Lingas, et al. (2013).

Hypobook 1: A high level of Neuroticism (NEO-FFI-3 N subscale T-score greater than 55) will be associated with concurrent tobacco cigarette use.

Rationale for Hypobook 1: Neuroticism was previously found to be negatively correlated with health behaviors; therefore, it was expected that e-cigarette users with high Neuroticism would continue smoking behavior during a cessation attempt.

Hypobook 2: A below average Self-Efficacy score (GSE score less than adult population mean score of 29) will correlate with concurrent tobacco cigarette use.

Rationale for Hypobook 2: Likewise for the rationale of hypobook 1, low Self-Efficacy or self-belief in the ability to achieve abstinence is likely to affect cessation success; therefore, both high Neuroticism and low Self-Efficacy were expected to be correlated with e-cigarette users' concurrent cigarette smoking.

Hypobook 3: A high level of Conscientiousness (NEO-FFI-3 C subscale T-score greater than 56) will correlate with no current tobacco cigarette use.

Rationale for Hypobook 3: Because Conscientiousness was positively correlated with health behavior, it was expected that an above average score in an individual's self-control and ability to resist impulses would have a correlation with smoking abstinence.

Hypobook 4: A high positive dimensions Hardiness score (an aggregate score greater than or equal to 36 on the DRS-II positive dimensions) will correlate with no current cigarette use.

Hypobook 5: A high negative dimensions Hardiness score (an aggregate score greater than or equal to 36 on the DRS-II negative dimensions) will correlate with concurrent cigarette use.

Rationale for Hypotheses 4 and 5: Because Hardiness represents stress resistance, it was expected that the stress of adopting e-cigarettes and abstaining from tobacco cigarettes would be resisted by individuals with high positive dimensions of Hardiness; therefore, these individuals would successfully reduce harm by not smoking. Alternately, it was expected that high scores in the negative dimensions of Hardiness would correlate with a failure to abstain.

Hypobook 6: Extremely Gritty individuals (those with a Grit-S total score of 5) will correlate to sustained smoking abstinence.

Rationale for hypobook 6: The highest percentile scorers on the measure of Grit represent individuals with the highest affinity for goal-orientation; therefore, these individuals were expected to sustain the longest periods of e-cigarette use without any smoking.

Research Design

The study design was cross-sectional and participation was voluntary and anonymous for all respondents. No identifying data was collected from respondents. Respondents were informed of this confidential nature and were instructed to discontinue at any time for any reason.

The survey was administered by the investigator by open call on the internet and direct solicitation at a variety of locations. Online solicitation utilized online forums for e-cigarette users. Volunteers who participated online were directed to the secure website www.surveymonkey.com. This website was employed because it offered security and confidentiality of data. Recruitment locations included e-cigarette stores and e-cigarette refill fluid stores across southern California.

Participants were initially presented an informed consent document (Appendix A) prior to responding to survey items, which described the purpose of the study as well as the demographics, personality assessment, and patterns of use questionnaires. The survey included FTND, GSE, DRS-II, and Grit-S scales, and NEO-FFI-3 N and C subscales. E-cigarette users were asked to volunteer in order to investigate the relationship between personality and e-cigarette use for smoking cessation. Upon reading the informed consent document, those participants providing assent were prompted to respond to all questions as quickly and accurately as possible. The survey and data collection was active until 200 surveys were completed without omissions.

Participants

A sample of 599 current e-cigarette users was recruited. The sample of convenience consisted of 85% male, 15% female e-cigarette users aged 18~72 years. Duration of use ranged from less than 1 month to multiple years. Participants were recruited from the following establishments: E-Cig Gallery Laguna Hills, Vapor Craze Irvine, E-Cig Emporium Irvine, and Vape First Tustin. Online participants were recruited from the following forums: www.e-cigarette-forum.com, www.vapingunderground.com, www.reddit.com/r/electronic_cigarette, and www.vaportalk.com.

Instrumentation

A survey was designed to assess nicotine dependence and personality factors of grit, self-efficacy, hardiness, neuroticism and conscientiousness as well as patterns of e-cigarette use. Two demographic items were included, age and gender.

Nicotine Dependence

In order to measure the extent of nicotine dependence, the Fagerström Test for Nicotine Dependence (FTND) was utilized. FTND consists of six items which assess time to first cigarette of the day, smoking in places where forbidden, the cigarette an individual would most hate to give up, cigarettes per day, smoking in the morning, and smoking if ill. Each item is scored based on response choices and the total ranges from 0 to 10. These scores correspond to dependence level ranging from very low by a score of 2 or less, low dependence with a score of 3-4, moderate with 5, 6-7 high, to 8-10 very high. Scores are positively correlated with nicotine levels and inversely related to abstinence (Cinciripini et al., 2003). FTND has acceptable internal consistency and is related to indices of smoking heaviness.

Grit

The Short Grit Scale (Grit-S) was utilized to assess Grit. The instrument consists of 8 items rated on a 5-point scale of not like me at all to very much like me. Grit-S items are scored half with ascending values and half descending. The composite score yields a rating of Grit from not at all gritty to extremely gritty. Duckworth and Quinn (2009) validated Grit-S with acceptable internal consistency of alphas ranging from 0.73 to 0.83 as well as confirmatory factor analysis. The scale was also found to be relatively stable over time.

Self-Efficacy

The Generalized Self-Efficacy Scale (GSE; Schwarzer & Jerusalem, 1995) was utilized in order to assess a sense of perceived Self-Efficacy. The instrument was designed to predict coping with daily stressors and adaptation after experiencing stressful life situations for the general adult population. It consists of 10 items rated on a 4-point scale and yields a composite score ranging from 10 to 40. The unidimensional scale has high reliability with Cronbach's alphas ranging from 0.76 to 0.90 and extensive criterion-related validity.

Neuroticism and Conscientiousness

In order to assess Neuroticism and Conscientiousness, the corresponding subscales of the NEO Five Factor Inventory (NEO-FFI-3) were utilized. NEO-FFI-3 is an inventory that represents the Five Factor Model. The Neuroticism and Conscientiousness subscales each contain 12 items rated on a 5-point scale of stdongly disagree to strongly agree. Costa and McCrae (1992) cited validity coefficient alphas ranging from 0.78 to 0.86, factor-scale correlation ranging from 0.94 to 0.97, and equivalence coefficients ranging from 0.90 to 0.93 for all subscales.

Hardiness

The measure of Hardiness was provided by the Dispositional Resilience Scale (DRS-II). The scale was developed as a short measure of Hardiness and consists of six subscales each with three items. Items are rated on a 5-point scale ranging from definitely false to definitely true.

The subscale domains are delineated into positive dimensions of control, commitment, and challenge which are associated with higher levels of Hardiness as well as negative dimensions of powerlessness, alienation, and rigidity which are associated with lower Hardiness. Sinclair and Oliver (2003) identified strong reliability and validity evidence for DRS-II supporting psychometric properties of internal consistency reliability, confirmatory factor analysis, and predictive validity of stress and stress-related outcomes.

Patterns of Use

The patterns of use items designed by Goniewicz, Lingas, et al. (2013) were employed to assess e-cigarette use behaviors. The items include duration of use as delineated along Transtheoretical Model of Change stages, daily use, daily frequency, time of first use of the day, nicotine level, and concurrent cigarette use. These items provide data which will be correlated with personality factors.

Data Processing

Data was analyzed with Statistical Package for Social Services (SPSS-18) computer software. The quantitative analysis consisted of correlational analysis utilizing crosstabulation and Pearson chi-square test. The intercorrelations among the personality factors and the overall relationships between them and the e-cigarette Patterns of Use variables was yielded. Expected outcomes were overall positive correlations of Self-Efficacy, Hardiness, Grit, and Conscientiousness as well as negative correlations of Nicotine Dependence and Neuroticism with each of the duration of e-cigarette use which was formulated to match Transtheoretical Model of Change stages, while the inverse of these correlations were expected for nicotine level and concurrent tobacco cigarette use.

Assumptions and Limitation in Method

One limitation of self-reported responses is the inability to verify data. The type of data notwithstanding, the breadth of the data was also limited to a small number of personality factors in the first place. There was an assumption that not only was the collected data accurate, but that the scrutinized variables encompassed a reasonably accurate impression of germane factors.

This limitation was addressed insofar as the regression analysis provided insight into the comparative significance of the personality factors, but not within the scope of the multitude of personological factors that have been identified. The study was bound to those factors that seemed most noteworthy. Additionally, the sample itself may not have been representative of the whole of e-cigarette users as it was a sample of convenience.

Ethical Assurances

The survey was minimal risk to participants. Although questions regarding cigarette use had potential to trigger emotional distress, this risk was determined to be unlikely; however, referral resources were included at the conclusion of the survey for interested respondents.

Participation was voluntary and the ability to withdraw was explicitly stated. Discontinuing the survey had no penalty. All survey data was anonymous, and responses will be confidential until destroyed. These research materials will be kept per APA guidelines for a minimum of 5 years.

Chapter Summary

The research design and method chapter outlined an overview of the study, its intent, and the means by which it would be conducted. The study procedure was detailed as were the data collection tools, that is, FTND, GSE, NEO-FFI-3 subscales, DRS-II, Grit-S, and patterns of use items. The purpose of this study was to determine personality factor correlates of smoking cessation efficacy among e-cigarette users.

Chapter 4: Analysis

Chapter Overview

The purpose of this study was to determine personality factor correlates of smoking cessation efficacy among e-cigarette users. The research questions examined were as follows:

1. Do identified personality factors impact smoking cessation efficacy among e-cigarette users?
2. Is there a particular personality structure associated with successful smoking cessation?
3. Are there personality factors that best predict the success of self-assisted quit attempts using e-cigarettes?

In order to collect research data, the FTND, GSE, NEO-FFI-3 C- and N-subscales, DRS-II, and GRIT-S scales were used along with a research-developed patterns of use survey.

Findings

The overall findings of the study were different than expected. It appeared that the placebo effect played a role, and that psychogenic factors played a role in efficacy of a cessation attempt. Only one personality factor of those identified was revealed to play a statistically significant role in this analysis. Details of the descriptive and inferential statistical results ensue.

Descriptive Statistics

Of those 599 participants who volunteered or were recruited, 296 were excluded for incomplete survey responses. A total of 303 respondents' surveys were used in the study (n = 303, completion rate = 50.58%). Descriptive statistics of the demographic information is provided in Table 2. Respondents ranged in age from 17 years to 72 years, the mean age being 31.64 years old. Female respondents composed 15.5% of the sample (n = 47) and males 84.5% (n = 256). Among the respondents, 4.6% had used e-cigarettes for one month or less (n = 14),

25.1% for 1-6 months ($n = 76$), and 70.3% used e-cigarettes for more than 6 months ($n = 213$). A majority of respondents, 86.5%, did not concurrently use cigarettes ($n = 262$), while 13.5% continued to smoke cigarettes concurrent with e-cigarette use ($n = 41$).

Table 2

Participant Demographics

		Percentage	*n*
Gender	Male	84.5	256
	Female	15.5	47
Stage of Change	Preparation	4.6	14
	Action	25.1	76
	Maintenance	70.3	213
Concurrent Cigarette use	Current Smoker	13.5	41
	Non-smoker	86.5	262

Nicotine dependence. As noted in Chapter 3, nicotine dependence was measured using FTND. Scores ranged across the entire scale (M = 4.75, SD = 2.526). The frequency of scores is provided in Table 3.

Grit. Grit was measured using Grit-S. Total scores range from 1.5 to 5 (M = 3.18, SD = 0.664). Score distributions are included in Table 3.

Self-Efficacy. GSE was utilized to measure self-efficacy. Scores ranged from 10 to 40 (M = 32.29, SD = 4.782). Frequencies of these scores are detailed in Table 3.

Neuroticism. The personality trait of Neuroticism was measured using NEO-FFI-3 N-subscale. Scores ranged from 26 to 75 (M = 53.83, SD = 11.516). A summary of the frequencies of these scores is included in Table 3.

Conscientiousness. The personality trait of Conscientiousness was measured using NEO-FFI-3 C-subscale. Scores ranged from 25 to 71 (M = 44.74, SD = 11.584). A summary of the frequencies of these scores is included in Table 3.

Hardiness. The DRS-II was utilized as a measure of hardiness. The positive dimensions scale on DRS-II ranged from 12 to 45 (M = 32.29, SD = 5.936). The negative dimensions scale ranged from 10 to 44 (M = 24.20, SD = 6.730). Table 3 contains further details of personality factor metricization.

Inferential Statistics

In order to examine intercorrelations between personality factors and smoking cessation efficacy, for each respondent the scores on each of the scales were dichotomized, whether or not the score fell within the high range of the instrument. For FTND, this consisted of scores greater than 5 per the scale; GSE, 30 or above; Grit-S greater than 3; on NEO-FFI-3 C- and N- subscales, scores greater than 55 and 56, respectively; and, on DRS-II scores scores above 27 on the positive dimensions or below 27 on the negative dimensions. Score conversions in this fashion enabled correlational analysis of whether or not there was a relationship to current smoking.

Crosstabulation of the personality factor variables was conducted in order to analyze the data in terms of concurrent cigarette smoking at each stage of change. These results were subjected to a Pearson chi-square test to determine significance.

Participants who reported being in the preparation stage of change with average or below conscientiousness were significantly less likely than those who scored high conscientiousness to have concurrent cigarette use [$\chi 2$ (1, n = 14) = 5.92, p = .015]. However, this result which contradicts previous research is likely an artifact of extremely small sample size, so much so that an insufficient number of preparation stage e-cigarette users were identified in order to consider it.

Table 3

Frequency of scores within significant ranges by Stage of Change

	Preparation (<1 month e-cigarette use)	Action (1-6 months use)	Maintenance (>6 months use)
FTND	28.6% (n=4)	40.8% (n=31)	41.3% (n=88)
GSE	64.3% (n=9)	75% (n=57)	80.8% (n=172)
Grit-S	50% (n=7)	44.7% (n=34)	61% (n=130)
NEO-FFI-3 C	28.6% (n=4)	19.7% (n=15)	18.8% (n=40)
NEO-FFI-3 N	21.4% (n=3)	57.9% (n=44)	38% (n=81)
DRS-II positive	92.9% (n=13)	75% (n=57)	82.2% (n=175)
DRS-II negative	64.3% (n=9)	68.4% (n=52)	62.9% (n=134)
Current smoker	28.6% (n=4)	22.4% (n=17)	9.4% (n=20)

Participants with less than six months e-cigarette use in the action stage who scored high on neuroticism were significantly more likely than those who scored average or below neuroticism to have concurrent cigarette use [$\chi 2$ (1, n = 76) = 8.27, p = .004].

Participants with more than six months of e-cigarette use in the maintenance stage who scored high on self-efficacy were significantly less likely than those who scored average or below GSE to have concurrent cigarette use [$\chi 2$ (1, n = 213) = 6.12, p = .013].

Did identified personality factors impact smoking cessation efficacy among e-cigarette users? Neuroticism and self-efficacy appeared to play roles in smoking cessation efficacy utilizing e-cigarettes. High neuroticism appeared to be related to concurrent cigarette use in the first six months of adopting e-cigarettes. High self-efficacy appeared to be related to sustained abstinence from smoking. Hypotheses 1 and 2 were supported. No significant relationships were found with hardiness and grit, as well as nicotine dependence. Hypobook 3, 4, 5, and hypobook 6 were not supported.

Was there a particular personality structure associated with successful smoking cessation? Low neuroticism and high self-efficacy, that is a low susceptibility to disruptive emotions and strong self-belief, were found to be the most significant configuration of personality traits that supported smoking cessation utilizing e-cigarettes.

Were *there personality factors that best predict the success of self-assisted quit attempts using e-cigarettes?* Self-efficacy had the richest support for predicting successful smoking cessation in the sample. Noteworthy was that nicotine dependence did not appear to mitigate this factor.

Additional Findings

There was a clear positive relationship between duration of e-cigarette use and the rate of concurrent smoking. The longer the duration of e-cigarette use, the less likely participants were to continue smoking. A majority of the sample had used e-cigarettes for 6 months or more and were not current smokers. In addition, the strongest concentration of e-cigarette users who vaporized liquid containing no nicotine (0mg) was identified in those with durations of use that was 6 months or greater.

Analysis of Design

The design of this study utilized one-time recruitment and call for volunteers. This single-pass approach did not allow for observation of change over time, rather examined momentary personality factor scores. Stronger relationships could be revealed by monitoring the efficacy of cessation attempts utilizing the same measures before and periodically during a quit attempt in order to better identify which participants had successful, sustained outcomes.

The criteria for inclusion was also broad. Any e-cigarette user was accepted into the study, so not all participants necessarily utilized e-cigarettes for smoking cessation although all users were formerly cigarette smokers. The study revealed a subset of the sample that is of interest for future research, those who utilize e-cigarettes with 0mg nicotine and therefore represent e-cigarette users who do not use nicotine, the primary psychoactive chemical in tobacco cigarettes.

Discussion

The analysis of the data collected supported previous research, especially of Gulzar et al. (2009), which described that Self-Efficacy plays a role in transforming behavior at an attitudinal level, also to a degree the research of Koelen and Lindström (2005) on empowerment. These connections were further reminiscent of research by Judge et al. (2002) seeking a common core construct with these dispositional factors as well as Neuroticism.

The first hypobook that a high level of Neuroticism would be associated with concurrent tobacco cigarette use was supported, as was the second hypobook that a below average Self-Efficacy score would similarly correlate with concurrent tobacco cigarette use. Significant relationships were identified supporting these hypotheses; however, hypobook 3 regarding the closely-related factor of Conscientiousness was not supported, nor were the remaining hypotheses regarding Hardiness or Grit. Rather than goal-orientation or stress-resilience, the most closely related factor in smoking cessation utilizing e-cigarettes appeared to be self-belief.

Summary

The purpose of this study was to determine personality factor correlates of smoking cessation utilizing e-cigarettes. A survey was designed measuring levels of identified personality factors related to smoking and health behaviors. These factors were Neuroticism, Conscientiousness, Self-Efficacy, Hardiness, and Grit as measured by, respectively, NEO Five Factor Inventory 3 (Costa & McCrae, 1992) N-subscale and C-subscale, the Generalized Self-Efficacy Scale (Schwarzer & Jerusalem, 1995), the Dispositional Resilience Scale

(Sinclair & Oliver, 2003), and the Short Grit Scale (Duckworth & Quinn, 2009), along with a research- developed survey of patterns of use. It was administered to 599 participants, and 303 surveys were analyzed after exclusion of incomplete submissions.

The results of the study supported a relationship between Neuroticism and cigarette smoking concurrent to e-cigarette use less than six months as well as between Self-Efficacy and no concurrent cigarette smoking after 6 or more months. Conscientiousness, Hardiness, and Grit were not significantly correlated with smoking cessation utilizing e-cigarettes. There was a broad trend in the data that e-cigarette users successfully quit smoking and maintained smoking abstinence.

Chapter 5: Summary, Conclusions, and Recommendations

Summary

The increasing prominence of e-cigarettes has been accompanied by claims that the devices are effective smoking cessation aids. Outcomes of multiple surveys, the present study included, have supported the observational and anecdotal claims. The focus of this study was to examine the personality factors related to successful smoking cessation utilizing e-cigarettes, in particular the traits of Neuroticism, Conscientiousness, Self-Efficacy, Grit, and Hardiness. Past research has supported these constructs as being related to the adoption of health behaviors.

It has been identified that e-cigarettes were mostly used as a long-term substitute to avoid harm associated with smoking and were reportedly effective even in highly-dependent smokers (Farsalinos, Romagna, et al., 2014). E-cigarettes eliminate the smoke toxicants responsible for nearly all smoking-related diseases; therefore, abuse liability is a moot point in the context of harm reduction (Polosa et al., 2013). Side effects of use appear to be minor, health benefits substantial (Farsalinos, Romagna, et al., 2014).

The process of smoking cessation has been delineated along the lines of the Transtheoretical Model Stages of Change. In this model intention and behavior are measured according to five stages of change, each with its own psychological tasks toward cessation (Procaska, Redding & Evers, 2002). The ability to achieve success in an attempt and sustain abstinence has been investigated in the context of health behaviors, and those dispositional traits that support the endeavor.

The present study aimed to determine psychological traits related to successful smoking cessation utilizing e-cigarettes. The procedural methods included a survey or patterns of use data along with measures of identified personality trait measures of Neuroticism and

Conscientiousness with the NEO Five Factor Inventory 3 (NEO-FFI-3) N- and C-subscales, Self-Efficacy with the Generalized Self-Efficacy Scale (GSE), Hardiness with the Dispositional Resilience Scale (DRS-II), and Grit with the Short Grit Scale (Grit-S).

Conclusions

Research related to the personality factors associated with successful utilization of e-cigarettes in smoking cessation is limited. The purpose of this study was to determine the relationship between identified personality traits and the stage of change for e-cigarette users.

The results of the study supported previous research pertaining to global factors of Neuroticism and its effect on health behavior as well as the role of Self-Efficacy in achieving health behavior goals. Previous research examining Hardiness and Grit in the contexts of smoking cessation, or addictive behavior, were not supported. Upon reflection of this analysis, motivations to use e-cigarettes and, by extension, to quit smoking affect cessation-related outcomes. Some users may adopt vaping as a harm-reducing replacement for smoking with no intention to decrease dependence on nicotine, while others may view the utilization of e-cigarettes as a means of eventual complete abstinence from nicotine and thus the need to smoke or vaporize at all. These divergent patterns of use undoubtedly impact measures of cessation efficacy.

According to the analysis, high Neuroticism was associated with concurrent smoking during the first 6 months or less of adopting e-cigarettes. This result supports previous research suggesting that high Neuroticism increases chances of relapse during cessation attempts. In addition, high Self-Efficacy was associated with less likelihood of concurrent smoking during 6 or more months of e-cigarette use. This finding is suggestive of the role of empowerment generated by the use of e-cigarettes in smoking cessation.

The analysis did not find significant relationships between Hardiness or Grit and concurrent cigarette use. This lack of statistical significance indicates that self-belief is more important to the success of e-cigarette utilization in smoking cessation than either stress-resistance or goal-orientation. It is probable also that the research design of Although it has been observed that e-cigarettes are a less efficient delivery method of nicotine than cigarette smoking (Vansickel, Weaver & Eissenberg, 2012), it appears that levels of nicotine users are able to imbrue in vapor are sufficient to offset the stress of withdrawal and cessation in the long-term.

Notwithstanding, a majority of participants in the present research did not concurrently smoke cigarettes and a majority of e-cigarette users also utilized the devices for 6 months or longer. These broad trends appear to support the use of e-cigarettes as a NRT. The efficacy of utilizing e-cigarettes toward eliminating dependence on nicotine, however, requires further research.

Recommendations

The use of e-cigarettes as an effective replacement therapy was supported, but this investigation revealed that it falls short of a reliable method of supporting cessation behavior. There appears to be little incentive for behavioral extinction in part due to the significant health benefits of adopting vaporizing over smoking which provides a median between abstinence and continued use. Dependence on nicotine did appear to be affected in a minority of e-cigarette users.

Future Research

Future research would benefit from examining the trajectory of cessation attempts using e-cigarettes, the personality factors related to success, and overall patterns of smoking cessation. Advantageous in this regard is the monitoring of e-cigarette use over time. The relationship between continued or prolonged use of e-cigarettes and smoking cessation is not well understood.

A particular subset of e-cigarette users is also noteworthy. Those who vaporize liquid with 0mg nicotine, i.e. users who do not deliver nicotine through e-cigarette use, represent a pattern of use that tends to develop with prolonged e-cigarette use. Examining the psychology of this population may provide insights not only into smoking cessation, but the behavioral aspects of addictive behavior. Such users do not utilize e-cigarettes for the chemical effects of nicotine nor does vaping appear related to the short halflife of nicotine, rather appear to vaporize for other reasons. The role of personality factors in this behavior may further develop divergent means of treating overt aspects of behavioral addiction.

Mental Health Clinicians

There appears to be support for successfully utilizing e-cigarettes in structured smoking cessation interventions. The use of e-cigarettes is an effective NRT that reduces harm from cigarette smoking. Toward cessation, the devices afford greater control over nicotine delivery. Despite these benefits, e-cigarettes do not affect motivation to quit smoking and may represent an alternative rather than a stepping stone to becoming smoke-free; nonetheless, because e-cigarettes can be used with no nicotine, this alternative may serve as an effective health behavior. Further research is needed to better understand the long-term consequences of e-cigarette use, so it cannot be considered a singular goal to vape instead of smoke; however, this research suggests that fostering such a belief, that a smoker may effectively replace cigarettes with e-cigarettes, may improve the ability to decrease or eliminate nicotine dependence.

www.ingramcontent.com/pod-product-compliance
Lightning Source LLC
Chambersburg PA
CBHW070646240926
51846CB00003BA/803
* 9 7 8 3 9 4 8 9 3 4 3 7 8 *